Brudders' Books

BRUDDERS
learns
The Joy of Saying Thank You

By K.A. Leigh   Illustrated by Derek Roberts

Copyright © 2021 Brudders' Books, Inc.

All rights reserved.
Published by Brudders' Books, Inc.

No part of this publication may be reproduced, stored in a retrieval system, or transmitted in any form or by any means, electronic, mechanical, photocopying, recording, or otherwise, without written permission of the publisher and copyright owner, except for use of quotations in a book review. For information regarding permission, please email Brudders' Books, Inc. at hellobrudders@bruddersbooks.com

Brudders Learns the Joy of Saying Thank You / Story by K.A. Leigh / Illustrations by Derek Roberts

ISBN: 978-1-7347983-3-3
Library of Congress Control Number: 2021920986

Printed in the United States of America
by Signature Book Printing
https://signature-book.com

First Edition January 2022
10 9 8 7 6 5 4 3 2 1

The illustrations were compiled using pen, ink, and watercolor.
Brudders ® is a registered trademark of Brudders' Books, Inc.

For information and resources visit
www.BruddersBooks.com

Dedicated to our families,

You saw something in Brudders from the beginning,
and you've been there for us every step of the way.
Thank you for your endless encouragement and support.
We love you so much.

You are our greatest blessing.

K.A. + Derek

Early in the morning,
in the woods outside Brudders' tree home...
The beautiful sun was rising,
and the squirrels were starting to roam.

Brudders strettttched himself out of bed and looked outside at this beautiful day...

For he had just made friends with the forest animals and couldn't wait to play.

Then **CHOMP CHOMP, TIMMMBBBERRR!**
What was that sudden sound?

Brudders grabbed his trusty binoculars
and took a careful look around.

It's the bunnies...

...and the beavers!

Picking carrots and chopping wood!

Brudders' tummy started rumbling. Those carrots looked so good.

Brudders ran out the door with his wagon, excited to join in the fun.

"Hi, Brudders! It's harvesting day for carrots.
Come on over. You must try one!"

"Hi, Camille. Hi, Kale. Hi, Lucy."
Brudders greeted them, his eyes growing wide.

Look at all those juicy carrots...Brudders couldn't wait to try.

Brudders picked one up and started chewing, **MMMMM!**
They were better than anything he had tasted before.

"We're glad you like them, Brudders.
Feel free to take some more!"

Brudders added a few more carrots to his wagon, though he didn't want to stop.

How generous and kind of the bunny sisters to share with Brudders their new carrot crop.

The bunnies went back to harvesting, but something seemed left unsaid…

And just as he was getting ready to leave, an acorn plopped down on Brudders' head!

Brudders squinted his eyes as he looked up in the sky.
Who do you think he sees?

Why, it's Zeke of course, watching over him, nestled in the trees!

"Oh, Brudddders!" Zeke called down to him. "There is something important you must know...

"It's a special phrase, it'll make someone's day, that you can tell the bunnies before you go."

"The special phrase is '**Thank you**.'
It's a way to show that you appreciate...

"And if you say it to someone when they do something kind,
it puts an instant smile on their face!"

"An instant smile?" asked Brudders astounded.
"Well, that sounds really cool!"

"Go ahead and try it," said Zeke.
"Wait till you see what the bunnies do."

"Excuse me, Camille, Kale and Lucy, there's something I would like to say...

"**Thank you** for all the carrots and inviting me over to play."

The bunnies stopped what they were doing, as smiles crept across their face...

They looked back up at Brudders and started jumping all over the place!

Brudders couldn't believe what he was seeing, how good the phrase **thank you** made them feel!

He shouted out loud, saying it again,
"**Thank you,** Lucy, Kale and Camille!"

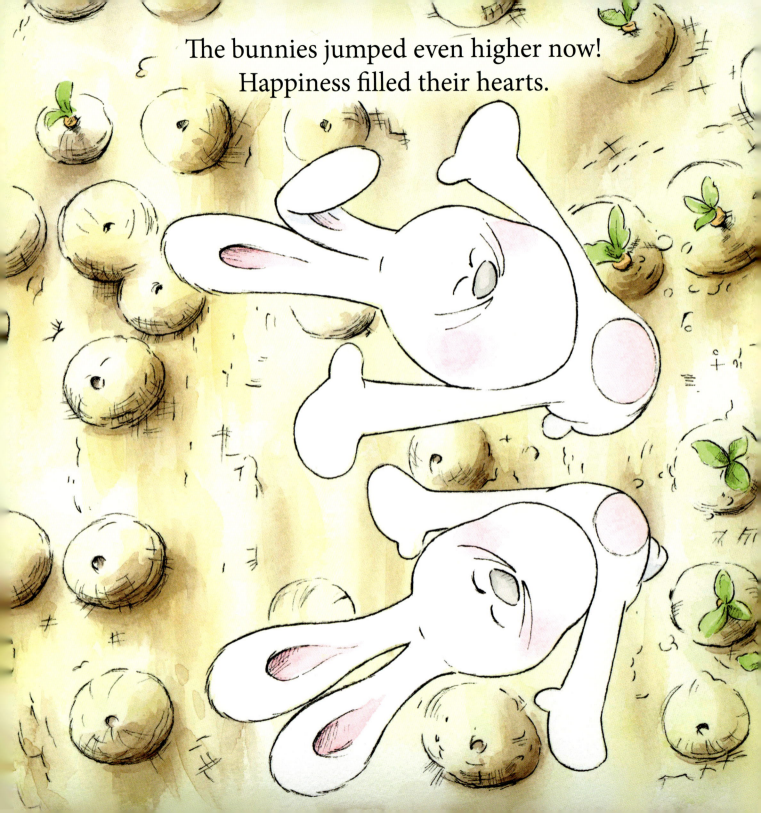

How wonderful it feels to know you are appreciated right from the very start.

Joy filled the forest as the sun was starting to set.

Brudders said **thank you** again to his forest friends, two words he'd never forget.

Brudders took his wagon full of carrots and started to head back home.

He was so grateful for this lesson Zeke taught him; otherwise, how would he have known?

Brudders said goodbye to Zeke,
but there was something he wanted to do...

He turned around with a big smile on his face
and said those two special words,
"Thank you."

Join Brudders In The Woods!

Learn more about the Brudders® series and download free activities and teaching resources at:

www.BruddersBooks.com

Meet Brudders' Creators

An author-illustrator couple on a mission to bring kids encouragement and hope as they grow through new lessons in life.

K.A. (Kristin) Leigh is a Florida-born animal lover with a passion for helping people through her writing. Once a 13-year career financial auditor and CPA, who has now turned breakthrough children's author, Kristin created the Brudders® book series to give kids a special friend they can relate to and lean on as they grow through different challenges in life.

Kristin was born and raised in Tampa, Florida, where she lives with Derek and their angel dogs, Jellybean and Brudders, who have since crossed the rainbow bridge.

Derek Roberts is a California-born illustrator and nature lover with a passion for painting imaginative worlds for kids. Admittedly, as a child, Derek would skip right over the words in his storybooks to immerse himself in the pictures instead.

Derek hopes his illustrations can paint stories that inspire children's minds to go into creative, joyful places like illustration books once did for him.